Copyright © 2021 by Williams Commerce

All rights reserved. No portion of this book may be reproduced mechanically, electronically, or by any other means, including photocopying without written permission of the publisher or author.

ISBN: 978-0-578-79806-6

Publisher

Williams Commerce, LLC

williamscommerce1.com

IG: @wcwriting1

NYA THE GREAT
And her visit to the Firehouse.

Story by
Mario Jackson

Edited by
William Jackson,
ABA, B.Acy., MBA

Illustrated by
Justin Dunn

To Kamaria and Khayla, my beautiful daughters, I hope I make you proud. Love Dad

Tiffanye S. Wesley
Deputy Fire Chief

Mario V. Jackson's Nya, The Great, is a brilliantly written work that is long overdue in the world of children's fiction. Nya The Great captures the unknown world of a female officer in the male-dominated profession of firefighting. A firefighter himself, Mario understands the vital role that women play in the Fire Service.

As the first woman promoted to Deputy Fire Chief in my department's 80-year history, I was as excited as Nya to take the journey to the firehouse to visit her aunt. Mario takes us on an unforgettable journey, one that most of us only dream about at night. We often have images of big red fire trucks, dalmatian dogs, and healthy male firefighters preparing a meal for the team. If ever, we seldom visualize a firehouse with beautiful, smart, and courageous women as firefighters or team leaders.

Allow the story of Nya, The Great to be more than a dream for your little one; allow it to be a story of a possibility that leads to reality just as it did for Mario's sister and just as it did for me! "Whatever your mind can Conceive and Believe, it can Achieve" Napolean Hill.

Nya didn't sleep a wink last night.
It's finally the day she's been waiting for, today is the day she is to visit her aunt who is a captain at the fire station.

Nya smiles from ear to ear, bursting with excitement as they walk to the fire station. To Nya, it seems as if it they'll never get there. Nya tries to run ahead but her dad holds tightly to her hand. "Slow down little one, we'll get there soon enough," dad says.

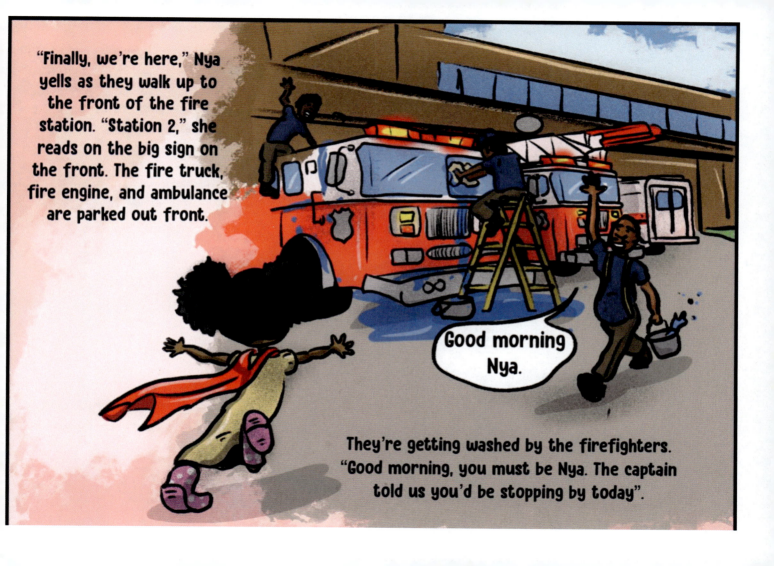

"You're just in time to help me with my morning checks. Are you ready?" "Yes," Nya screams. "That's awesome. Jump up in the fire engine and tell me if you see everything I call out to you".

Equipment List

"Do you see my flashlight?" "Check," Nya says. "What about my walkie talkie?" "Check," Nya again says. Nya then points to something on the seat and says, "Auntie what is this? It looks like a mask for divers." "Well Nya, that helps breathe when I go into fires. It's very important, without it I can't do my job safely."

Other firefighters check their equipment as well. The driver checks all the lights on the engine and firefighters who ride in the back check their tools, like the axe and ceiling hooks. "We make sure our tools and equipment are clean and ready for use," one of the firefighters says to Nya.

"Follow me to the office," Nya's aunt says, as they walk through the big building. "We have to practice things we may have to do during emergencies. We call these drills and we practice every day so we won't forget. If it's okay with you, I'm going to give you a few drills you can practice with your family at home to help keep everyone safe." "It's okay," Nya responds.

Nya's aunt gives her a list of three items for which she is up for the task:
(1) Change the batteries in a<u>ll</u> the smoke detectors,
(2) Agree on a safe place to meet outside if there's a fire, and
(3) Make sure windows and doors aren't blocked by trash or large boxes.

"Nya, I've got something very special for you," her aunt says as she opens a closest door in the office. "Here's a new fire helmet for you just like the one I wear."

Nya is excited to receive her new helmet. To her, it's the coolest helmet she's ever seen. It's red with yellow stickers, very shiny, and best of all fits just right. As soon as she puts it on, she feels like a real firefighter. Nya couldn't be happier.

While walking home, still smiling from her visit to the fire station, Nya and her dad hear sirens in the distance. As the noise of the sirens becomes closer, they realize it's firefighters from Station 2.

As the fire engine passes by, Nya's aunt gives her a wink from the front seat, and Mr. Lewis blows the horn. "Yup, still loud," Nya yells to her dad over the noise of the sirens.

The End

Every day, the once impossible dreams of little girls from the past are now becoming the realities of women of today. Keep accomplishing goals and breaking barriers. You inspire more than you know.

Made in the USA
Coppell, TX
09 April 2021

53436670R00017